Uncharted, Unexplored, and Unexplained

Scientific Advancements of the 19th Century

Samuel Morse

and the Story of the Telegraph

Mitchell Lane
PUBLISHERS

P.O. Box 196
Hockessin, Delaware
19707

Uncharted, Unexplored, and Unexplained

Scientific Advancements of the 19th Century

Titles in the Series

Visit us on the web: www.mitchelllane.com
Comments? email us: mitchelllane@mitchelllane.com

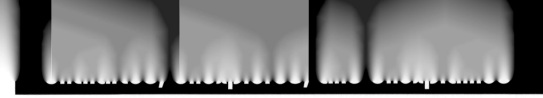

Uncharted, Unexplored, and Unexplained

Scientific Advancements of the 19th Century

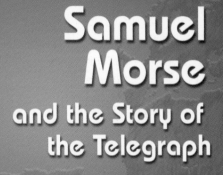

Samuel Morse

and the Story of the Telegraph

by Susan Zannos

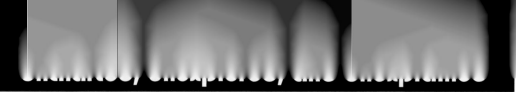

Scientific Advancements of the 19th Century

Mitchell Lane
PUBLISHERS

Printing   2   3   4   5   6   7   8
     Library of Congress Cataloging-in-Publication Data
Zannos, Susan.
     Samuel Morse and the electric telegraph / Susan Zannos.
          p. cm. — (Uncharted, unexplored, and unexplained)
     Includes bibliographical references and index.
     Contents: A long way from home—A young artist—Hard times—Success at last—The telegraph.
     ISBN 1-58415-269-9 (Library bound)
     1. Morse, Samuel Finley Breese, 1791-1872—Juvenile literature. 2. Inventors—United States—Biography—Juvenile literature. 3. Telegraph—United States—History—Juvenile literature. [1. Morse, Samuel Finley Breese, 1791-1872. 2. Inventors. 3. Artists.] I. Title. II. Series.
TK5243.M7Z36 2004
621.383'092—dc22   2003024138

ABOUT THE AUTHOR: Susan Zannos has been a lifelong educator, having taught at all levels, from preschool to college, in Mexico, Greece, Italy, Russia, and Lithuania, as well as in the United States. She has published a mystery *Trust the Liar* (Walker and Co.) and *Human Types: Essence and the Enneagram* (Samuel Weiser). Her book, *Human Types*, was recently translated into Russian, and in 2003 Susan was invited to tour Russia and lecture about her book. Another book she wrote for young adults, *Careers in Education* (Mitchell Lane) was selected for the New York Public Library's "Books for the Teen Age 2003 List." She has written many books for children, including *Chester Carlson and the Development of Xerography* and *The Life and Times of Ludwig van Beethoven* (Mitchell Lane). When not traveling, Susan lives in the Sierra Foothills of Northern California.

PUBLISHER'S NOTE: This story is based on the author's extensive research, which she believes to be accurate. Documentation of such research is contained on page 47.

The internet sites referenced herein were active as of the publication date. Due to the fleeting nature of some web sites, we cannot guarantee they will all be active when you are reading this book.

Scientific Advancements of the 19th Century

Samuel Morse

and the Story of the Telegraph

*For Your Information

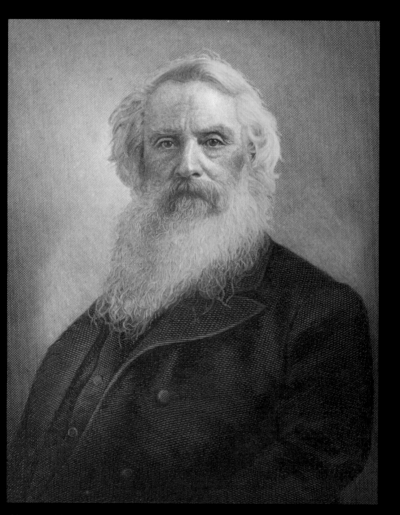

Not until late in his life did Samuel Morse achieve the success he struggled so hard to achieve—and that success did not come in his chosen career as an artist. Fame and fortune came as the result of his work in developing a practical method for sending messages over long distances. The telegraph that he developed spread rapidly over the entire planet, making Samuel Morse a wealthy man.

1

A Long Way From Home

Fourteen passengers left New York harbor aboard the ship *Lydia* on July 13, 1811. They were bound for Liverpool, England. One of the members of the group was a pleasant and handsome young man of cheerful good spirits. He enjoyed making sketches of the other passengers for their amusement. His name was Samuel Finley Breese Morse.

Samuel was on his way to London to become an artist. He had left behind his parents and his two younger brothers. He already missed his family long before land was sighted after 20 days at sea. It took six more days before the ship approached Liverpool. A storm was raging, and a crowd had gathered at the dock. Samuel wrote in his journal, "By far the greater part of the crowd had hastened to see us dashed against the head of the wharf by the fury of the tide."[1]

Whether or not that was actually true, it did seem that the English were a bit hostile. The day after landing, Samuel went to the mayor of Liverpool to get permission to travel on to London. The mayor told Samuel that he had 10 days to leave town. If he was found in Liverpool after that, he would be put in jail.

Samuel Morse was aware of the tensions between America and England. The Revolutionary War, America's war of independence from

England, had ended in 1783. More than two decades later, it was still in the minds of many people in both countries. Although America had won her freedom, problems remained. There were border disputes between the new nation and Canada, which was still an English colony. English warships were searching and seizing American merchant ships.

When he got to London and found a place to stay, he wrote to his parents, "I only wish you had this letter now to relieve your minds from anxiety. . . . I can imagine mother wishing that she could hear of my arrival, and thinking of thousands of accidents which may have befallen me. I wish that in an instant I could communicate the information; but three thousand miles are not passed over in an instant, and we must wait four long weeks before we can hear from each other."[2]

The young artist, who at this time had hardly a single thought of anything other than learning how to paint, would eventually make the sending of messages thousands of miles in an instant a reality. But he had a long hard road to travel first.

Samuel had come to England with another American painter, Washington Allston, who had already begun teaching him. In London, Allston introduced Samuel to Benjamin West, a famous painter of historical scenes. West was also an American, but he had lived in England for many years and was the head of the Royal Academy. He was a friend of noted English painters like Thomas Gainsborough and Sir Joshua Reynolds.

In addition to being a famous artist, Benjamin West was a kind and generous man. He took time to teach young artists. Gilbert Stuart, who would become the most famous of all the American portrait painters, worked in West's studio for five years. Even though West was now 74 years old, he greeted his young countryman Samuel warmly and accepted him as a student.

Samuel's goal was to be admitted to the Royal Academy. To be considered, he had to submit a drawing to a panel of judges. Samuel finished the drawing and showed it to West, who said it was a good start. Samuel had thought his drawing was finished, but he took it home

Washington Allston (left) was a well-known American artist who became the friend and teacher of young Samuel Morse at the beginning of his art studies. They traveled together to London where Allston introduced Morse to the famous painter Benjamin West (right). West, who was then head of the Royal Academy, accepted Samuel Morse as his student.

and worked on it some more. He showed it to West again. Again he was told to finish it. Not until he had worked on the drawing for three months did his teacher say it was ready for the judges. The extra effort paid off. Samuel was admitted to the Royal Academy and began studying seriously.

In June of 1812, the British government changed their policy of searching American ships. This had been one of the reasons the Americans were angry. Samuel and his American and British friends celebrated. They thought that there would be no war. But they were wrong. There was no way to get the news across the Atlantic in less than a month. At the urging of President James Madison, the U.S. Congress declared war before receiving the news that the British policies had changed. The War of 1812 had begun. It was a war that never should have happened.

Samuel Morse worked hard to develop his artistic ability. When Allston urged him to make a figure in clay before starting a painting of the dying Greek hero Hercules, he followed the suggestion. Both Allston and West praised the sculpture. West told Samuel to send it to an art show, where it won first prize and earned a gold medal for Samuel. The large painting he did of Hercules also earned praise.

Samuel wrote to his father that he would soon be making money. He was wrong. He received praise and encouragement, but no one bought his paintings. His father had to continue sending him money to live on for the four years he studied in England.

Meanwhile the war with England continued in America. Many battles were fought. The British invaded Washington and burned the White House. Finally, on December 24, 1814, the Treaty of Ghent was signed, ending the war. Samuel Morse and his friends celebrated again, thinking at last there was peace between their two countries.

The Battle of New Orleans began on January 8, 1815. More soldiers were killed in this battle than in any other battle of the War of 1812, but the battle was fought over two weeks after the war was over.

It took a month for news of the treaty to reach the United States. On January 8, 1815, British soldiers attacked New Orleans. General Andrew Jackson and his American soldiers fought bravely. Over 2,000 men were killed in this battle that occurred after the war had been over for more than two weeks. The War of 1812 had begun after the reason for it no longer existed. The biggest battle of the war, with the greatest loss of life, was fought after the war had ended. Again Samuel Morse thought about how much human suffering could be avoided if only there was a faster way to communicate across long distances.

Ancient Signals

Samuel Morse wasn't the only person to think about long distance communication. For several millennia, people had tried to solve the problem. Even the best human messengers—running, riding swift horses, or crossing the ocean—could take weeks or even months to reach far-off destinations.

Fire was one of the oldest methods. When the Greeks attacked Troy over 3,000 years ago, the Greek King Agamemnon arranged a system of signal fires. When Troy was captured after 10 years of fighting, the king lit a fire. Watching on an island, another man saw the glow and lit his fire. Seeing this fire, still another watcher lit a third fire—and so the news traveled across the Aegean Sea to the mainland. Finally it reached a watchman on the roof of the king's palace. He rushed below to inform the queen.

Fire signals only worked at night, and only on clear nights. American Indians used fire during the day by putting green wood on the flames to create smoke. They made a kind of language from the smoke by creating pauses with a blanket over the fire.

Another daytime method of sending messages was by reflecting the sun's rays with polished metal or mirrors. Again the process depended on the weather—if you had to send a message on a rainy day, you were out of luck.

Some American Indian and African tribes used drums to send signals. They had quite complex drumming languages. Hearing drums in the jungle at night could be a frightening experience for those who did not know the language but suspected that it meant trouble.

Arm signals, or signals with flags called semaphores, could be used to spell out messages over short distances. Each flag position represented a different letter. Before the invention of the electric telegraph, a series of stations were set up within sight of each other. This system is still used in the military when it is necessary to keep radio silence.

Samuel Morse was not only the inventor of the Morse code, but also an artist. Although he had difficulty selling his paintings during his lifetime, he is now considered a major American painter, and his work is on display in art museums. Morse painted this picture called *Otsego Lake From Apple Hill* in 1829. He was among many artists to paint a scene of Otsego Lake, which is located in east-central New York.

2

A Young Artist

Samuel Finley Breese Morse was born in Charlestown, Massachusetts, on April 27, 1791. His family was highly respected and probably rather stuffy. His father, the Rev. Jedediah Morse, was minister of the First Congregational Church in Charlestown. He became famous for the geography books he produced. He knew many of the founding fathers of the United States, including George Washington and Benjamin Franklin. Samuel's mother, Elizabeth Finley Morse, also came from an influential family. She was the granddaughter of the president of Princeton College. Jedediah and Elizabeth had 11 children, but only three sons grew to adulthood. The oldest of the boys was Samuel.

Well-educated, well-read, and kind, the minister and his wife frequently entertained well-known people. One of them later wrote, "An orphan myself, and never having a home, I have gone away from Dr. Morse's house in tears, feeling that such a home must be more like heaven than any thing of which I could conceive."[1]

Samuel's two younger brothers added to the family honors. His brother Sidney entered Yale when he was 11 years old. He went on to a successful career as an inventor and, with his younger brother Richard, publisher of the *New York Observer*. Richard entered Yale when he was 14 years old and graduated when he was 18. He mastered Latin, Greek, and Hebrew, as well as French and German and several other modern languages.

In a family like that, someone had to be the black sheep. Samuel took on that responsibility. As his first biographer put it, "He manifested in early childhood and in youth a beautiful playfulness, and fondness for amusements, that were never checked by his parents."[2] In other words, Jedediah and Elizabeth had a lot of patience. They needed it.

The Morse family was a close and happy one. From left to right in this family portrait are Samuel's mother, Elizabeth Finley Morse, Samuel, his father Jedediah Morse, and his two brothers, Sidney and Richard. The globe represents Jedediah's career as a writer of books about geography.

When Samuel was four years old he was sent to a preschool. At that time Sidney was one year old and Richard a newborn infant, so his mother had her hands full. The old woman who ran the little school was crippled and unable to leave her chair. She kept order with a long switch. Children who caused trouble would be pinned to her dress with a large safety pin.

Young Samuel showed his interest in art early. He took a pin and drew a portrait of the old woman by scratching it into her chest of drawers. As a result he was pinned to her dress. As he struggled to get free the dress ripped. Her next method of dealing with the young artist was a switch across his bottom.

In 1799, Samuel's parents next sent him to a preparatory school in Andover, Massachusetts. This school was to prepare him for Phillips Academy, which in turn would prepare him for Yale College. In a letter to Samuel when he was nine years old, his father gave a lot of advice about letter writing—and offered to show him letters from George Washington that could serve as a model.

In the same letter, Jedediah Morse also said to his son, "Your natural disposition, my dear son, renders it proper for me earnestly to recommend to you to attend to one thing at a time; it is impossible that you can do two things well at the same time, and I would therefore never have you attempt it. . . . I expect you will read this letter over several times, that you may retain its contents in your memory. . . . If you improve, I shall be encouraged to give you more advice, as you may need it."[3]

Jedediah Morse and his wife Elizabeth Finley Morse, shown in these portrait paintings, both came from highly respected and influential families. Jedediah was minister of the Congregational Church in Charlestown, Massachusetts, and was also a well-known writer of geography books. Of their eleven children only three sons lived to become adults. Samuel Morse was the oldest of their three boys.

Whether or not Samuel memorized his father's letter is not known. In his own letters he told about some of his activities. Few of them related to his studies.

One of these activities was art. His father had mixed feelings. On one hand, he praised his son's talent to friends, emphasizing that he was self-taught. He also promised rewards such as paint boxes and books for good behavior. Yet Jedediah emphasized that the primary purpose of art was for amusement.

In 1805, Samuel completed his studies at Phillips Academy and entered Yale College. As a sophomore, he represented his class at a trial in which the college cooks were found guilty of "crimes" such as "concealing pies which belonged to the students, having suppers at midnight, and inviting all their neighbors and friends to sup with them at the expense of the students."[4]

Samuel helped to construct an 18-foot-long balloon out of letter paper. The young men suspended it from a tower on the Yale campus, filled it with hot air, and set it loose. At first the balloon's flight was successful. Then it blew against a building, caught fire, produced a brilliant blaze, and ended up a pile of ashes.

Aside from making sure the cooks didn't eat the pies that students would like to have and amusing himself and others with dramatic experiments, Samuel Morse did attend classes. He was not much interested in most of his studies. One thing that did appeal to him was the newest sensation in science: electricity. He thought that it was at least as exciting as a paper hot air balloon.

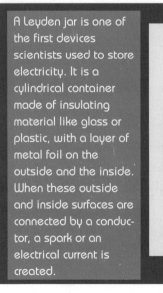

A Leyden jar is one of the first devices scientists used to store electricity. It is a cylindrical container made of insulating material like glass or plastic, with a layer of metal foil on the outside and the inside. When these outside and inside surfaces are connected by a conductor, a spark or an electrical current is created.

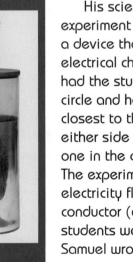

His science class did an experiment with a Leyden jar, a device that could store an electrical charge. The teacher had the students stand in a circle and hold hands. The boy closest to the Leyden jar at either side touched it. Everyone in the circle got a shock. The experiment showed that electricity flowed through a conductor (and also that the students were conductors). Samuel wrote to his parents:

This tuned circuit transmitter (left) was developed by Marconi in his experiments with radio waves. It contains a Leyden jar and a spark-gap. The oscillator spark-gap (right) was invented by Augustus Righi, Professor at the University of Bologna. A high voltage controlled by Morse key transfers to the central spark-gap completing the circuit.

"I never took an electric shock before; it felt as if some person had struck me a slight blow across the arms."[5] This was one lesson that Samuel Morse would remember later in his life.

He didn't remember many of his other lessons. Just as in preschool when he had been pinned to his teacher's dress, he was mostly interested in drawing. At Phillips Academy and Yale, he fidgeted and doodled during classes. He was barely able to wait for them to be over so he could get back to his drawing and painting. He wanted to be an artist.

At Yale, Samuel started earning a little money by making sketches and paintings of his classmates and professors. They would pay him five dollars for miniature paintings on ivory and a dollar for a profile. It wasn't much, but it helped. His father had three sons in college at the same time, on a clergyman's salary. Any extra income was appreciated.

His mother and father kept hoping that Samuel would become interested in "respectable" studies. They wanted him to be a doctor or lawyer, or a clergyman like his father. Samuel disappointed them. When he graduated from Yale at the age of 19, he was ready to begin studying art. He wrote home, "As to my choice of profession, I still think that I was made for a painter, and I would be obliged to you to make such arrangements with Mr. Allston, for my studying with him."[6]

If Allston accepted young Samuel as his student, it would be a great opportunity. Allston was not just a good artist. He was well-known in both England and America. His friends included the famous poets Samuel Taylor Coleridge, William Wordsworth, and Robert Southey, and the great English portrait painter Sir Joshua Reynolds.

There was only one catch. His father had other ideas. He wanted his son to start working with one of the companies that published his geography books. Samuel swallowed his disappointment.

"I was determined beforehand to conform to his [his father] and your will in everything,"[7] he wrote to his mother. But he wasn't completely happy with the decision. "I have been extremely low-spirited for some days past, and it still continues,"[8] he added.

This commemorative coin medallion was one of the many honors Samuel Morse received. His first successful attempt in sending a message from Washington to Baltimore on May 24, 1844 proved that the telegraph was a practical method of communicating over long distances. Soon afterwards telegraph lines spanned the globe, and Morse was acclaimed as the father of telegraphy.

Have you ever seen a portrait by American painter Gilbert Stuart? You have when you look at a dollar bill. The picture of George Washington is one of Stuart's portraits of our first president. Stuart was the most important portrait painter in America at the end of the 18th century. He painted over 1,000 portraits of presidents (Adams, Madison, and Jefferson, as well as Washington), military heroes, judges, and other leaders of the new nation.

George Washington by Gilbert Stuart

Stuart was born in Rhode Island in 1755. His artistic talent was obvious from an early age when a wealthy doctor, William Hunter, commissioned him to paint a picture of his spaniels. Hunter also introduced him to visiting Scottish artist Cosmo Alexander. When Gilbert was 15, he went with Alexander to Scotland.

When Alexander died suddenly in 1772, Stuart worked his way home and continued to paint portraits. Before the American Revolution began, Stuart traveled to London. He was accepted as an assistant to the famous painter Benjamin West, and spent five years in West's studio finishing up the master's portraits.

Gilbert Stuart

Stuart's successful career began in 1782 with "The Skater," a painting exhibited at the Royal Academy. From then on he had no trouble receiving commissions for portraits. Unfortunately, he always spent more than he earned and had financial difficulties all of his life. He married and had a large family of 12 children to support. He left London in 1787 and went to Ireland to escape his debts. Six years later he left Ireland for the same reason and arrived in New York in 1793.

Stuart's career flourished in the United States until his death in 1828. In an era before photography, painted portraits were the only pictures of themselves that people could have. Gilbert Stuart's paintings are brilliant masterpieces. They hang in the most prestigious museums in the world.

Samuel Morse was one of the earliest photographers. Unable to make a living with his painting, Morse learned the process of making Daguerreotypes from Louis Daguerre in Paris. He later opened his own Daguerrotype studio in New York to support himself while he developed the telegraph. Early photography required the subject to sit very still for a long time because long exposure times were necessary to fix the image.

3

Hard Times

Samuel's "career" in bookselling lasted just three months. Allston convinced Samuel's parents to allow the young man to accompany him to London. With Allston as his teacher and friend—the friendship would last throughout their lives—Samuel Morse was ready to begin his chosen career.

After four years of studying art in London, Samuel Morse returned to America. He was sure he would be able to sell his paintings and make money. He was wrong. He opened a painting studio in Boston—his father paid the rent—but he did not receive any orders for paintings. Samuel wanted to paint large, important historical paintings like the ones for which Benjamin West was famous. But Americans didn't have any use for that kind of painting. They wanted pictures of themselves. So Samuel painted portraits.

He started traveling from one large city to another, hoping to earn money by painting portraits. Wherever he went, people who knew his father welcomed him and provided him with a place to stay.

While he was traveling through New Hampshire in the summer of 1816, he stopped in Concord. There he met Lucretia Walker. The two fell in love and were married on September 29, 1818. Samuel had had his greatest success as a portrait painter in Charleston, South Carolina, so the young couple settled there. The city council of Charleston commissioned Morse to paint a portrait of the President of the United States, James Monroe. It was one of his most famous paintings.

But glory did not pay the rent. Samuel could not make enough money to support a family, especially when his daughter Susan was born in 1819. In what became a regular pattern, Lucretia and Susan went to live with Samuel Morse's parents while he continued traveling. Eventually he began to have some success. In 1822 he painted a large group portrait of all the members of the House of Representatives. Early in 1825 he received an important commission: painting the portrait of the French general the Marquis de Lafayette. He had been one of the heroes of the Revolutionary War by helping the American cause.

At last Samuel's career appeared to reach a point where he would be able to support his family in their own home. Lucretia wrote him an encouraging letter, saying, "The time is not far distant when you can be happy in the bosom of your much loved family, and that your dear children [Charles had been born in 1823] can enjoy the permanent advantage of an affectionate father's counsel and care."[1] He paid a quick visit to her, seeing his new baby James Edward Finley. Then he left for Washington, D.C. He wrote a long letter to Lucretia describing all the exciting things he saw.

The reply didn't come from Lucretia. It came from his father. It contained terrible news. His wife had died suddenly from a heart attack. It took two days for the message to reach him, and by the time he returned home Lucretia had been buried. Once again Samuel Morse felt the suffering that resulted from the inability to communicate over long distances.

Eventually, Samuel decided to return to Europe. He knew that four murals were to be painted on the walls of the U.S. Capitol building in Washington. He wanted to be one of the artists chosen to paint them. He thought that if he received more training from European artists, he would have a better chance of being chosen. He left his two sons with his brothers, and his daughter with Lucretia's sister, and sailed again for Europe late in 1829.

Samuel Morse was well-known in Europe, and respected as an artist. His friends included most of the famous writers and painters of the time. One of them was another American, James Fenimore Cooper. Cooper, the first popular American novelist, was living in Europe and became one of Samuel Morse's closest friends. The two Americans traveled together, and when they were apart wrote long letters to each other describing their experiences. Both were close friends of Lafayette, whose portrait Morse had painted.

Morse visited France and Italy and Switzerland as well as England. In France he not only painted, but also became fascinated with the French semaphore telegraph system. This system had been invented at the end of the 18th century by the Chappe brothers. It used a series of tall posts with movable arms at the top that were operated by pulleys. A different position of the arms stood for each letter of the alphabet. Soon the Chappes interested the French government in their system.

Each semaphore machine was operated by a man who observed the message from the previous station through his telescope. He then passed the message on to the next station. Using this method, a message could travel from Paris to the far southwestern corner of France in 40 minutes.

Claude Chappe, one of the brothers, had wanted to name their invention the "tachygraphe." That comes from two Greek words which mean "fast writer." A friend suggested "telegraphe," or "far writer."

According to writer Lewis Coe, "By 1844, France was crisscrossed with 5,000 kilometers [about 3,000 miles] of line having 533 stations. Telescope making became a profitable business because every semaphore station needed at least one! Although extremely slow compared to the electric telegraph that was to come later, the Chappe system achieved some results that were little short of miraculous for that time."[2]

Samuel Morse booked his passage on the *Sully* to return to America in 1832. On one of the first days of the voyage, the dinner table conversation was about electricity. A passenger was talking about the length of a wire wrapped around a magnet. Another passenger asked a question about how fast the electricity traveled through the wire. The answer was that experiments by Franklin had shown there was no difference in time between touch at one end of a wire and a spark at the other.

In an instant a spark jumped in Morse's mind. He said, "If the presence of electricity can be made visible in any part of the circuit, I see no reason why intelligence may not be transmitted instantaneously by electricity."[3]

Samuel Morse was not a scientist. He thought he was the first one to have this idea. Perhaps if he had known how many scientists were already working on this idea, he never would have tried it himself. But he didn't. He spent the rest of the voyage of the *Sully* developing the ideas that would become the telegraph. He filled his sketchbooks with page after page of notes and drawings. These books, and the testimony of the other passengers, were important later when there were legal conflicts over patents for the telegraph.

Morse's idea was brilliant, not just because of his grasp of science but also because of the simplicity of the code he created. He realized that he had three elements to work with: an electrical current, a way of breaking the electrical current, and the amount of time the current was flowing. Therefore, he could build the alphabet out of three things: a dot (or quick touch of current), a dash (or longer flow of current), and the pauses between them. The Morse code was born.

Others before him had tried sending messages with electricity, but their systems were too complicated. One used a separate wire for each letter of the alphabet—a charge applied to a wire caused a ball at the other end to move. Another system used only one wire, but the electricity activated complicated dials that turned to display the proper letter. These early attempts used static electricity, which wasn't reliable. Only

INTERNATIONAL MORSE CODE

A	•—	N	—•	1	•————	Ñ	——•——	N with tilde
B	—•••	O	———	2	••———	Ö	———•	O with umlaut
C	—•—•	P	•——•	3	•••——	Ü	••——	U with umlaut
D	—••	Q	——•—	4	••••—	,	••——••	comma
E	•	R	•—•	5	•••••	.	•—•—•—	period
F	••—•	S	•••	6	—••••	?	••——••	question mark
G	——•	T	—	7	——•••	;	—•—•—	semicolon
H	••••	U	••—	8	———••	:	———•••	colon
I	••	V	•••—	9	————•	/	—••—•	slash
J	•———	W	•——	0	—————	-	—••••—	dash
K	—•—	X	—••—	Á	•——•— A with accent	'	•————•	apostrophe
L	•—••	Y	—•——	Ä	•—•— A with umlaut	()	—•——•—	parenthesis
M	——	Z	——••	É	••—•• E with accent	_	••——•—	underline

The International Morse Code was the brilliant idea of Samuel Morse. It was this alphabet constructed from dots and dashes that made it possible to transmit messages over long distances with electrical current. The other systems that had been tried before the Morse code was created were too complicated for practical use.

after the type of current generated by batteries was developed could electricity be useful for communication.

In England, William Cooke and Charles Wheatstone would establish a needle telegraph using five needles that pointed to letters on a circular dial. When three of the five lines broke down, the operators quickly devised their own code with the two remaining needles. Later it was discovered that only one needle and one dial were needed. Many 19th century scientists, and many practical workers like the operators who quickly devised their own codes, prepared the way for the success of the Morse telegraph.

Meanwhile, on the *Sully*, Samuel Morse could hardly wait to reach America. As he left the ship he said to the captain, "Well, Captain, should you hear of the telegraph one of these days, as the wonder of the world, remember the discovery was made on board the good ship *Sully*."[4]

Samuel's brothers Richard and Sidney met him at the dock. He immediately told them of his idea. His brothers, who had for a long time worried about Samuel and his inability to make money, felt hopeful. The idea sounded good. Richard had already invited Samuel to live with him and his family, an invitation Samuel gratefully accepted.

This Morse key was a lever that the telegraph operator pushed down to complete the electrical circuit. To produce a dot the key was pushed down quickly, while to produce a dash the key had to be held down longer.

The Morse tape inker base contains a spool of paper tape that passes under the brass plate and takes the pressure of the inking. It is run by impulses from the wireless receiver and produces a visible record of Morse code.

Another version of the Morse key was called the "Grasshopper" because of its shape. It acted as a send and receive switch.

This field transmitter was used by the Army. It had a Leyden jar capacitor and was powered by an induction coil where the Morse key was mounted.

James Fenimore Cooper

James Fenimore Cooper was the first major American novelist. He was born in 1789 in Burlington, New Jersey. His parents were hard-working Quakers who became wealthy developing land. As a boy James developed a love of nature and wilderness that would be expressed in his best novels.

After being educated in the village school, James went to Yale. In his junior year he was expelled. Among other jokes, he had trained a donkey to sit in a professor's chair. Like many young men who weren't serious about their studies, young Cooper joined the navy. His experiences serving on U.S. ships later inspired his stories of the sea.

When his father died in 1809, Cooper inherited the family property and became a farmer. He married in 1811. He had always liked reading. One day after finishing an English novel he decided he could write a better story. His wife encouraged him and he started writing. His first novel, Precaution, was modestly successful. The second novel was an adventure story about the American Revolution entitled The Spy. The hero was a spy for George Washington. That book brought Cooper fame and wealth. He gave up farming and devoted his time to writing.

Cooper was a prolific writer who produced over 35 novels and other books such as critical and political essays. His most successful novels were about the adventures of a woodsman, Natty Bumppo (who was also called Leatherstocking or Hawkeye), and his Indian companion Chingachgook. These novels included The Deerslayer and The Last of the Mohicans. They continue to be popular and have been made into several movies.

Between 1826 and 1833 Cooper and his wife lived in Europe where he was a good friend of English novelist Sir Walter Scott, the Revolutionary War hero Marquis de Lafayette, and Samuel Morse. Before his death in 1851, Cooper became more and more distressed about the wasting of forests and other wilderness areas. He was one of America's first outspoken conservationists.

After the success of the telegraph, Samuel Morse received honors from all over the world. He received a gold medal from the American Institute, the Prussian golden medal for scientific merit, the cross of the Order of Dannebrog in Denmark, the great gold medal of science and art from the Emperor of Austria, the Knight of Tower and Sword from Portugal, and honorary degrees from many universities.

4

Success at Last!

Morse set to work immediately to construct the telegraph. Since all the materials that he instantly had available were his artists' supplies, that's what he used. These included a picture frame and a canvas stretcher. He molded lead pieces in the fireplace in his brother's living room, spilling melted lead on his sister-in-law's carpet. His invention worked.

Morse's biggest problem was still money. When he returned from Europe, he became a professor of painting and sculpture at a new school that would become New York University. He made so little money teaching that he had to live at the school. He wasn't doing much better with his art. He did not receive the commission he wanted for one of the paintings in the Capitol Rotunda even though he was one of the most respected painters in America. The blow ended his hopes that his career in art would be successful if only he continued to work hard at it.

Ironically, long after Samuel Morse's death, his paintings were finally recognized as masterpieces. Today, museums and galleries collect his paintings. Special exhibits of his work draw large crowds of art lovers. One of Morse's largest paintings, "The Gallery of the Louvre," was virtually ignored when he completed it in 1833. In 1982, that painting

These four paintings by Samuel Morse show the range of his subject matter: portraits and group portraits, landscapes, and architectural studies. He is now regarded as a major American painter. His paintings hang in important museums and are prized by collectors, but he was unable to make a living from his art during the years of his active painting career.

sold for $3,250,000. It was the highest amount of money ever paid for an American painter's work up to that time.

But when he desperately needed to earn a living from his painting, he couldn't. He turned all of his energies to developing his invention. It would be 12 long, hard years from the voyage of the *Sully* to the first success of the telegraph.

Today if you want to buy the materials necessary to make a tele-graph, all you have to do is stop by the nearest hardware store. You can buy long rolls of insulated wire, switches for turning electricity on and off, and dozens of different types of batteries.

In 1835 there were no such things for sale. Samuel Morse had to make everything himself. Wire did not come in rolls. He had to buy pieces, join them together, and insulate the wire by wrapping it in cotton. At first he couldn't make his device work. One scientist wrote about him, "He found himself so little acquainted with the subject of electricity that he could not make his simple machine operate through the distance of a few yards."[1]

Morse was not trained in science. Fortunately, a chemistry professor at the university, Dr. Leonard Gale, became interested in Morse's efforts. Morse had been using only one battery. Professor Gale told him to use 20 batteries. Gale also pointed out that the magnet Morse was using was too weak because there were too few coils of wire around it. Morse used 10 miles of wire wound tightly around reels and strung around the room. With a stronger electric current, his device worked.

In 1837 Morse held his first demonstration in his classroom at the university. He invited rich people who—he hoped—would invest in his invention. Only one man seemed interested. He was Alfred Vail, a student who had formerly been in Morse's art classes. Vail was good at mechanics. Although he didn't have money, his family was wealthy and owned an iron works. Vail offered to help construct better equipment in return for a share of the telegraph patent.

Vail was a big help. The apparatus was redesigned and constructed more professionally. After applying for a patent for the telegraph and giving several more demonstrations of his equipment, Samuel Morse went back to Europe to try to get patents there. In England he saw the telegraph invented by Cooke and Wheatstone. The English patent office protected its own inventors and told Morse that America should be big enough for him.

In France he got a patent. It was useless unless he could get a line operating within two years, which he couldn't. The only profit from this

European trip was meeting Louis Daguerre in Paris and learning Daguerre's photographic process. This process produced Daguerrotypes, an early type of photograph that soon would put many portrait painters out of business.

To make money while he was working on his telegraph, Morse opened his own Daguerreotype studio in New York when he returned to the United States in 1840. Two years later, Samuel Morse and the men helping him, Professor Gale and Alfred Vail, planned another demonstration. They laid a cable under New York Harbor. They published notices in the newspapers promising a public demonstration the following day. A message would be sent through underwater cable.

According to Kenneth Silverman, "A crowd gathered to watch Morse send a message electrically through a mile of water. He got off several characters, but without warning the transmission went dead. A merchantman had been getting underway, and its anchor fouled the submerged cable. As Morse looked on, the ship's crew hauled in two hundred feet of his carefully insulated copper cable and severed it. The crowd scattered—with jeers, by one account. Humiliated by his abrupt and complete failure in public, Morse was unable to sleep."[2]

By now, he had been working on his invention for more than 10 years. Unless he could show that it could send messages over a long distance, no one would be interested in it. But he could not do that without money. And he couldn't get money unless people were interested in it. It was a vicious circle. His only hope was the United States government.

Early in 1843, the House of Representatives in Washington, D.C., passed a bill granting $30,000 to test Morse's electric telegraph. All that remained was for the Senate to pass the bill also. But there was a great deal of business before the Senate. The last day of the session was March 3. Samuel Morse sat in the gallery of the Senate all day and part of the night. Friends told him there was no chance of his bill being voted on before the session ended at midnight. Discouraged and depressed at one more failure, Morse returned to his hotel.

The next morning a young lady named Annie Ellsworth greeted him with a big smile. "I have come to congratulate you!"[3] she said. Morse didn't know what she was talking about. She told him that the bill granting $30,000 for an experimental telegraph line had been voted on in the Senate just before midnight. It had passed! Samuel Morse was overjoyed at the news. He promised Annie that she could choose the first message to be sent over his telegraph.

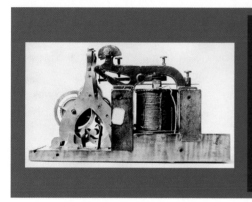

Morse's partner, Alfred Vail, produced this Morse telegraph register receiver. A stylus operated by an electromagnet (the tightly wound wires make it look like a spool of thread) marked dots and dashes on a paper tape. Vail and Morse had an agreement by which all of their inventions would carry Morse's name even though Vail invented them.

At last Morse and his partners had the money to prove that the telegraph could send messages instantly over long distances. They planned to lay an underground wire between Washington and Baltimore. The distance was about 40 miles. But their troubles were far from over.

A great deal of the underground cable was in the ground when Morse discovered that the electrical signals were not getting through. He dug up a section of cable and found that the insulation had burned off because the pipe the wire was in had gotten too hot. He tried a different kind of pipe. It didn't work either. He had already spent $23,000 of the $30,000 appropriation. Only $7,000 remained. Morse didn't know what to do.

Alfred Vail urged Morse to string the wires on poles. They ordered the poles and started construction. They didn't know how to insulate the wires where the poles held them up. They knew that glass was a good insulator, so they used broken bottlenecks for the wire to pass through at the top of each pole. Finally they were ready.

This picture captures the historic moment when Samuel Morse sent the first message by telegraph between Washington and Baltimore. It was this demonstration that began the spread of telegraph wires over the entire world. Because Morse held the patents for the telegraph, each telegraph company had to pay him.

On May 24, 1844, officials and friends of Morse gathered in the chamber of the U.S. Supreme Court. Morse had his equipment there. In Baltimore, 40 miles away, Alfred Vail was in the train station with his equipment. Between them stretched the telegraph wires that they had struggled with such difficulties to put up.

The crowd was excited. Samuel Morse seemed the calmest person in the room. Annie Ellsworth presented the message she had chosen, "What hath God wrought!" Although Morse had not seen the message before, he believed that the telegraph was God's work. Slowly and steadily he tapped out the words in the Morse code he had created.

Moments after he had finished the message, the identical message came back from Baltimore. The witnesses were astonished. Everyone cheered and clapped. They all crowded around to congratulate Morse.

At last people understood what Morse had known since that first moment of inspiration aboard the *Sully* 12 years before. The telegraph was an invention that would change the world.

This first model of a telegraph was made in Samuel Morse's art studio in 1835, using a canvas stretcher, homemade battery, and wooden parts. The wooden arm sliding across the metal saw tooth generated the code. This created dots and dashes that were printed out on the paper tape.

FYI**nfo**

Louis Jacques Daguerre was an artist in Paris who created a huge theater, the Diorama. It featured large painted scenes that seemed to change with different lighting. He worked hard to make the scenes look as real as possible.

Daguerre learned about another man, Joseph-Nicephore Niepce, who was creating plates that could be exposed to light and then inked and printed. In 1826 Niepce made an eight-hour exposure of the view from his window. It was the world's first photograph! Daguerre

Louis Daguerre

and Niepce became partners. Unfortunately, Niepce died before they were successful, but Daguerre had learned enough to continue by himself.

Joseph-Nicephore Niepce

Daguerre developed a method of treating silver-plated copper sheets with iodine. This made them sensitive to light. He then exposed the plates in a camera. He developed, or fixed, the images with mercury vapor. He called his invention the Daguerreotype. A member of the French Academy of Sciences was so enthusiastic that he convinced the French government to compensate Daguerre directly and give the invention to the world. The steps of the process were publicized on August 19, 1839.

Soon Daguerre's instructions were translated into a dozen languages, and Daguerreotypes were in demand all over the world. At first it was only possible to make images of buildings and landscapes because the exposure time was so long. Improvements in the lenses and chemicals soon reduced the exposure time and made portraits possible, although the person had to sit very still for several minutes.

daguerrotype camera

Daguerreotypes became particularly popular in the United States after Samuel Morse introduced them in New York. Portraits were no longer exclusively for the rich. Now anyone with five dollars could have his or her face and figure reproduced on a piece of silver, covered with glass, and presented in a leather case. By the middle of the 19th century, millions of Daguerreotypes had been made. They are still collected and exhibited by those who are interested in charming old photographs.

Samuel Morse is shown here with an early design of a telegraph register. It was made by J. W. Norton, the first telegraph manufacturer, who was on the first board of directors of the Magnetic Telegraphic Co. Although Morse did not continue to make developments, he controlled the patents for the telegraph and was honored as "the father of the telegraph."

5

The Telegraph

The patents for the telegraph made Samuel Morse a wealthy man. There were several court battles over the patents, but Morse won them all. Everyone who wanted to establish a telegraph line had to pay him for the use of his invention. Aside from that, Samuel Morse and the telegraph went their separate ways. Like a grown child that no longer needed the support and protection of a parent, the telegraph began a life of its own.

As one historian put it, "Morse lived to see himself honored as the father of the telegraph, yet in many ways his contribution was minimal. He was not a scientist or a mechanic, and not a very good businessman. Nevertheless, he gave the world a successful telegraph system when all the others, better qualified, were muddling around with impractical schemes."[1]

After the first telegraph message had been sent between Washington and Baltimore in 1844, use of the telegraph to send messages long distances in both America and Europe increased rapidly. Within four years, telegraph wires connected every state east of the Mississippi River, with the exception of Florida. By 1852, more than 23,000 miles of telegraph wires had been erected in the United States.

This model uses the basic features of the 1844 telegraph receiver used to send the message between Washington and Baltimore. It accompanied an application for a patent, which was granted as patent number 6,420 on May 1, 1849, in which Samuel Morse described the method for making dots and dashes on paper.

Not surprisingly, people had already begun to think about connecting the North American continent to Europe with an undersea cable to carry messages. But the long distance and the depth of the sea were big obstacles. It wasn't until early in 1857 that manufacture of the first cable began. In August of that year, two ships loaded with cable left Valentia Harbor in Ireland to lay the cable. Six days later the cable snapped with only 380 miles of cable laid. The ships had to return to port.

The second try began the following June. The two ships met each other in mid-Atlantic and joined the two ends of cable. It broke. They tried again and made 40 miles before it broke again. Then they managed to lay 146 miles before it broke a third time. The ships returned to Ireland where they decided they had enough cable left for one more try. They again went to the mid-point of the ocean and spliced their cables. This time the attempt was successful. On August 5, 1858, Ireland and Newfoundland in North America were joined by telegraph cable.

As Tom Standage writes, "The celebrations that followed bordered on hysteria. There were hundred-gun salutes in Boston and New York; flags flew from public buildings; church bells rang. There were fireworks, parades, and special church services. Torch-bearing revelers in New York got so carried away that City Hall was accidentally set on fire and narrowly escaped destruction."[2]

Unfortunately, the celebrations proved somewhat premature. Apparently the engineer in charge used voltages that were too high when he began sending the messages. Within a few weeks, the line stopped functioning. In 1866, the steamship *Great Eastern* laid a cable that proved to be reliable. Undersea telegraph cables increased rapidly from then on, linking all parts of the world.

In this artist's rendering, the steamship *Great Eastern* is shown with her crew laying the cable for the first successful undersea cable linking the United States with Europe in 1866. Prior to this there had been many failed attempts in which the cables broke or ceased functioning.

Meanwhile, back in the United States, efforts were focused on a telegraph line that would span the continent. By 1860, telegraph lines from the east had reached as far west as Omaha, Nebraska. In California lines went as far north as Sacramento and east to Carson City, Nevada. About this time, the Pony Express began operating. Relays of horseback riders could take letters from St. Joseph, Missouri, to Sacramento in about 10 days. A telegraph could shorten that time to a matter of seconds.

Construction was delayed because the wire and insulators had to travel from New York around Cape Horn to San Francisco. On May 27, 1861, a construction gang left Sacramento and headed east. They had difficulty getting through the Sierra Nevada Mountains because of all the wagon trains headed west on the narrow roads. They didn't get to Carson City, where the actual construction began, until late June.

The crew in the east started west from Omaha. They set the first pole on July 4, 1861. There were some problems. One was that buffalo liked to scratch their backs on the telegraph poles. The great shaggy beasts would frequently knock the poles over. Another problem was attacks by hostile Indians. But even so the construction of the telegraph line across the United States took only four months. The estimate had been that it would take two years.

The construction crews used Pony Express riders to communicate with each other. As one historian said, "The Pony Express continued until the line was complete. Then the colorful horsemen passed into history."[3]

By the time the line was completed, the Civil War had started. One of the first messages from California sent to President Abraham Lincoln said in part, "The people of California desire to congratulate you upon the completion of the great work. They believe that it will be the means of strengthening the attachment which binds both the East and West to the Union...They regard the Government with affection, and will adhere to it under all fortunes."[4] During the actual fighting, both North and South made extensive use of the broad network of wires in their respective territories.

During all the time that the telegraph was spreading out around the earth like an enormous spider web, Samuel Morse had been enjoying the money it earned for him. In 1847, he bought a large estate in New York called Locust Grove. It included 100 acres and overlooked the Hudson River. The following year, Samuel Morse attended a family wedding and saw his cousin, Sarah Griswold. He hadn't seen Sarah since she was a girl. Now she was 26 years old and very beautiful. Even though Samuel was 56 and some people disapproved of the relationship because of the difference in their ages, the two were married within two months.

When Sarah was accused of marrying Morse for his money, she replied, "Oh, I wish he was poor, and I would then let him know whether I loved him."[5] When they asked her what she would do if he suddenly lost all his property, she answered, "What would I do? Why, support him with my own hands."[6] It was a very happy marriage.

In 1851, Samuel and Sarah Morse enlarged and remodeled the house at Locust Grove. Its twenty-four rooms provided plenty of space for their growing family, which eventually included four children. It also provided an opportunity for Samuel's grown children to finally live at least briefly with their father. The couple also had a home in New York City. In 1866, Samuel, Sarah, and their children traveled to Europe, where they spent two years.

Samuel received honors and awards from many countries around the world. One of them was the dedication of a statue of himself in New York's Central Park on June 10, 1871. He was 80 years old. That evening, a special banquet was held in his honor. The master of ceremonies was William Orton, the president of Western Union. By that time, it was the dominant telegraph company in the United States.

The evening's highlight came at 9:00 P.M. Standage writes, "All the telegraph wires of the United States were connected to a single Morse key, on which Morse himself bade farewell to the community he had created. 'GREETINGS AND THANKS TO THE TELEGRAPH FRATERNITY THROUGHOUT THE WORLD. GLORY TO GOD IN THE HIGHEST, ON EARTH PEACE. GOOD WILL TO MEN,' ran the message, transmitted by a skilled operator, after which Morse himself sat down at the operating table to tremendous cheers, which were silenced by a gesture from Orton. In total silence, Morse then tapped out his signature, 'S.F.B. Morse,' and the entire audience rose to its feet in a standing ovation. When the applause and cheering finally died down, Orton said, 'Thus the father of the Telegraph bids farewell to his children.' "[7]

On April 2, 1872, Samuel Morse died after a brief illness. The telegraph flashed the news of his death around the world.

The telegraph was the world's most important method of communication for half a century or more. Then other ways of sending messages began to take over. Things like the telephone, radio, and now satellite television have taken over the business of broadcasting information and entertainment.

An old telegraph operator from the Midwest still dreams going into his old Western Union office. He taps out "C" for Chicago, and then "G" for Galesburg. There is no answer. "No one ever will answer now because it is a dream, a dream of people, places, and events that are gone forever. . . . The great network of telegraph wires that once enfolded the nation like a cobweb has vanished just as surely as the spider's handiwork is erased by a sudden sweep of the broom."[8]

41

During the last half of the 19th century and the first half of the 20th, telegraph operators were in demand, just as computer programmers are today. Most were self-taught. Their first task was memorizing Morse code, the dots and dashes that stood for letters of the alphabet and numerals. After that, they spent hours and hours practicing sending messages. It was harder to get practice receiving messages unless two people were learning together and could take turns.

The telegraph had not been in operation long when it became clear that the telegraphers did not need to translate the printed dots and dashes to words. They could understand the messages immediately! Just as a child learns language by hearing it, the telegraph operators found they could understand the sounds of Morse code directly.

Teenagers who wanted to be telegraphers would hang out in the telegraph office or railway station. They would do errands for the operator. Sometimes when the operator needed a break they would get a chance to operate the sending keys. When messages came in they could practice writing them down. When they got good enough, they might get a job as a relief operator.

Telegraphers knew everything that went on in the town they lived in— business deals, social events, personal triumphs, and tragedies. Sometimes operators were heroes. In the disastrous Johnstown Flood of 1889, telegrapher Hettie Ogle remained at her post, sending reports and warnings until the dam actually broke. She drowned as the mountain of water swept through Johnstown.

Press telegraphers were the best in the business. They not only knew Morse code but also mastered the Phillips code invented in the 1880s. Phillips code used about 3,000 symbols for English words and phrases. A good Morse operator could send about 30 to 40 words per minute. A Phillips operator could double that speed because he did not have to spell out all the words.

Even though the job of telegrapher no longer exists, many amateurs still enjoy learning Morse code and sending and receiving messages by radio or telephone lines.

Chronology

1791 Born on April 27 in Charlestown, Massachusetts
1795 Sent to preschool near his home
1799 Begins attending preparatory school at Andover
1805 Is admitted to Yale College
1810 Graduates from Yale
1811 Sails to England to study painting with Washington Allston and Benjamin West
1815 Returns to America; opens a painting studio in Boston without success
1818 Goes to Charleston, South Carolina, where he achieves some success painting portraits; marries Lucretia Walker
1819 Daughter Susan is born
1823 Son Charles is born; Lucretia and the children live with Samuel's parents while he travels to develop his painting career
1825 Son James is born; Lucretia dies
1829 Leaves children with relatives and sails for Europe to study art
1832 Has the idea for the electric telegraph on return voyage to America
1835 Appointed art professor at New York City University
1837 Conducts successful demonstration of the telegraph; Alfred Vail becomes partner
1838 Returns to Europe to try, without success, to get patents for his telegraph there
1839 Meets Louis Daguerre and learns the process of making Daguerreotypes
1843 U.S. Congress approves bill granting $30,000 for construction of telegraph line
1844 Completes telegraph line from Washington, D.C., to Baltimore, Maryland, and sends first message: "What hath God wrought!"
1845 With partners, forms The Magnetic Telegraph Company; returns to Europe to interest countries in using his telegraph system
1847 Purchases Locust Grove, the estate on the Hudson River that will be his home
1848 Marries his cousin, Sarah Griswold, with whom he will have four children
1866 Travels to Europe for two years
1871 Honored with statue in Central Park, New York
1872 Dies at his New York home on April 2 after a short illness

Timeline of Discovery

1738	Painter Benjamin West is born in Springfield Township, Pennsylvania.
1752	Benjamin Franklin flies a kite during a thunderstorm and proves that lightning is electricity.
1791	English scientist Michael Faraday, who makes many discoveries about the nature of electricity, is born.
1794	The Chappe brothers establish a semaphore telegraph line from Paris to Lille in France.
1815	English semaphore telegraph links London with Chatham.
1837	Charles Wheatstone and William Cooke establish an electrical telegraph on the London and Birmingham Railway in England.
1838	The first message using dots and dashes for letters of the alphabet is sent.
1848	The Associated Press is formed.
1850	Sound reading replaces tape registers for receiving telegraph messages.
1851	The New York and Mississippi Valley Printing Telegraph Company is formed; it later becomes Western Union.
1858	The first transatlantic cable is laid but fails after 24 days.
1860	Automatic repeaters enable telegraph lines to operate over long distances.
1861	The transcontinental telegraph line is completed.
1866	The Great Eastern lays a transatlantic cable that proves to be successful.
1872	Joseph Stearns patents the duplex telegraph, which allows two messages to be sent on one wire.
1874	Thomas Edison invents the quadruplex telegraph, allowing four messages to be sent over one wire.
1876	Alexander Graham Bell invents the telephone.
1879	Walter Phillips invents the Phillips Code for press telegraphy.
1881	The Postal Telegraph Company is organized.
1904	Horace Martin introduces the Vibroplex automatic key.
1928	Postal Telegraph and Mackay System become part of International Telephone and Telegraph (IT&T).
1930	The Associated Press closes its last Morse line.
1933	Western Union introduces singing telegrams.
1945	The Postal Telegraph Company becomes part of Western Union.
1960	Western Union sends its last Morse telegram.
1988	The Western Union Telegraph Company is reorganized as Western Union Corporation and concentrates on loan services and monetary transactions.
2004	The symbol @, using .__._., officially becomes part of the Morse code.

44

Chapter Notes

Chapter 1   A Long Way from Home

1. Samuel Irenaeus Prime, *The Life of Samuel F.B. Morse* (New York: Arno Press, 1974), p. 31.

2. Ibid.

Chapter 2   A Young Artist

1. Samuel Irenaeus Prime, *The Life of Samuel F.B. Morse* (New York: Arno Press, 1974), p. 8.

2. Ibid., p. 13.

3. Ibid., p. 15.

4. Ibid., p. 17.

5. Ibid., p. 22.

6. Ibid., p. 25.

7. Kenneth Silverman, *Lightning Man: The Accursed Life of Samuel F.B. Morse* (New York: Alfred A. Knopf, 2003), p. 16.

8. Ibid.

Chapter 3   Hard Times

1. Kenneth Silverman, *Lightning Man: The Accursed Life of Samuel F.B. Morse* (New York: Alfred A. Knopf, 2003), p. 72.

2. Lewis Coe, *The Telegraph: A History of Morse's Invention and its Predecessors in the United States* (London: McFarland & Co., Inc., 1993), p. 6.

3. Samuel Irenaeus, Prime, *The Life of Samuel F.B. Morse* (New York: Arno Press, 1974), p. 252.

4. Coe, p. 27.

Chapter 4   Success at Last!

1. Lewis Coe, *The Telegraph: A History of Morse's Invention and its Predecessors in the United States* (London: McFarland & Co., Inc., 1993), p. 29.

2. Kenneth Silverman, *Lightning Man:The Accursed Life of Samuel F.B. Morse* (New York: Alfred A. Knopf, 2003), p. 216.

3. Samuel Irenaeus Prime, *The Life of Samuel F.B. Morse* (New York: Arno Press, 1974), p. 465.

Chapter 5   The Telegraph

1. Lewis Coe, *The Telegraph: A History of Morse's Invention and its Predecessors in the United States* (London: McFarland & Co., Inc., 1993), p. 36.

2. Tom Standage, *The Victorian Internet* (New York: Walker and Company, 1998), pp. 80–81.

3. Coe, p. 39.

4. Coe, p. 46.

5. Coe, p. 35.

6. Ibid.

7. Standage, pp. 186–87.

8. Coe, p. vii.

Glossary

cable (KAY-bul)—a strong rope of wire.

commission (kuh-MISH-un)—business entrusted to a person.

estate (es-TAYT)—property such as land and the buildings on it.

exposure (ex-POE-sjur)—in photography, the time film is subjected to light.

instantaneous (in-stun-TAYN-ee-us)—immediate; at once.

insulator (IN-suh-layt-ur)—a material that prevents the flow of energy such as heat or electricity.

miniature (MIN-yut-chur)—a very small painting, usually done on ivory.

mural (MEW-rul)—a very large painting done on a wall.

novelist (NAH-vul-ust)—someone who writes long works of fiction.

portrait (POR-trayt)—painting of a particular person.

profile (PRO-fyel)—side view of the face; a drawing of this side view.

reel (REEL)—cylinder for winding up wire or string.

semaphore (SEM-uh-for)—signaling device using movable arms, flags, or lights.

session (SESH-un)— sitting of an assembly for legal business.

transatlantic (trans-ut-LAN-tik)—crossing the Atlantic Ocean.

transcontinental (trans-kon-ti-NEN-tul)—crossing a continent.

treaty (TREE-tee)—formal agreement between nations.

For Further Reading

For Young Adults:

Alter, Judy. *Samuel F.B. Morse: Inventor and Code Creator.* Chanhassen, Minnesota: The Child's World, 2003.

Hudson, John. *Samuel F.B. Morse: Artist With a Message.* Fenton, Michigan: Mott Media, 1987.

Kerby, Mona. *Samuel Morse.* New York: Franklin Watts, 1991.

Latham, Jean Lee. *Samuel F. B. Morse, Artist-Inventor.* Broomall, Pennsylvania: Chelsea House, 1991.

Quackenbush, Robert. *Quick, Annie, Give Me a Catchy Line!: A Story of Samuel F. B. Morse.* Englewood Cliffs, NJ: Prentice-Hall, Inc., 1983.

Works Consulted:

Coe, Lewis. *The Telegraph: A History of Morse's Invention and its Predecessors in the United States.* London: McFarland & Co., Inc., 1993.

Prime, Samuel Irenaeus. *The Life of Samuel F.B. Morse.* New York: Arno Press, 1974.

Silverman, Kenneth. *Lightning Man:The Accursed Life of Samuel F.B. Morse.* New York: Alfred A. Knopf, 2003.

Standage, Tom. *The Victorian Internet.* New York: Walker and Company, 1998.

On the Internet:

Samuel Morse Timeline – Biography of Samuel Morse
http://inventors.about.com/ library/inventors/ bl_morse_timeline.htm

Samuel F.B. Morse Biography Locust Grove National Historical Landmark
http://www.morsehistoricsite. org/

Gilbert Stuart Birthplace
http://www.geocities.com/ Heartland/Hills/6365/ stuart.html

Daguerre, Louis Jacques Mande
http://www.rleggat.com/ photohistory/history/ daguerr.htm

The James Fenimore Cooper Society
http://external.oneonta.edu/ cooper/

Index